General Directions

FABRICS
Our cover models show an array of framed pieces. Six are stitched on 14-count fabrics and one is stitched on 16-count Aida. You can choose any background you wish, but be sure to cut the fabric large enough to contain the design and allow ample margins for your desired finishing.

THREADS
The Anchor, J. & P. Coats, and DMC embroidery floss colors are specified by number in the Color Keys. Each company has its own color range, so these suggestions are not perfect color matches; alter them as desired. Cut thread into comfortable working lengths—we suggest about 18".

Generic color names are given for each floss color in a design; for example, if there is only one green it will be so named, but if there are three greens, they would be labelled lt (light), med (medium), and dk (dark).

Specialty threads are also used for contrast and interest in the Panther design on pages 8-9. Balger 1/16"-wide ribbon, a flat metallic tape, provides contrasting color and sparkle. Flower thread has a matte finish; use your favorite brand. Metallic thread is also made by several companies; choose the one you find most comfortable to work with.

MISCELLANEOUS SUPPLIES
Size 24 or 26 blunt-pointed tapestry needles are suitable for 14- and 16-count fabrics. Use a hoop or not, as you prefer. If you do, choose a clean small plastic or wood hoop with a screw-type tension adjuster. Small, sharp embroidery scissors are handy; do not use them on paper.

CHARTED DESIGNS
Each square on a chart represents the space in which a Cross Stitch or a Half Cross Stitch can be made. The symbol in a square specifies the color to be used as noted in the Color Key. If the color name appears without a preceding symbol and equal sign, the color is only used for one of the following decorative stitches. Backstitches and Straight Stitches are indicated by straight lines, Couching is represented by a crosshatched line, and a French Knot is shown by a dot.

Each Color Key specifies the floss color(s) used and special stitching information. The number of stitches in width and height are given, and centers are shown by arrows. If a chart is too large for one page, the continuation chart has two shaded rows that repeat the last two rows of the previous page; the shaded area is for reference only and not to be stitched.

GETTING STARTED
Unless otherwise directed, work design centered on fabric. Follow arrows to find center of charted design; count threads or fold fabric to find its center. Count up and over to the left on chart and fabric to begin cross stitching.

To begin, bring threaded needle to front of fabric. Hold an inch of the end on the back, then anchor it with your first few stitches. To end threads and begin new ones next to existing stitches, weave through backs of several stitches.

THE STITCHES
Note: Unless otherwise noted in the Color Key, use two strands of floss or thread for all cross stitching and French knots, and one strand for all backstitching, straight stitches, and couching.

Cross Stitch
To make a Cross Stitch, bring thread up at 1, down at 2, up at 3, down at 4, to complete the stitch. Work horizontal rows of stitches, **Fig 2**, wherever possible. Bring thread up at 1 and continue numerical sequence, working half of each stitch across the row and completing them on the return.

Half Cross Stitch
This partial stitch is used when working with 1/16" ribbon (Panther design, pages 8-9). Follow numerical sequence to work only the first half of a cross stitch. Work the first horizontal row from left to right, the second row from right to left, **Fig 3**; continue in this manner.

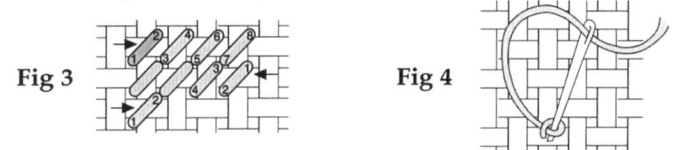

French Knot
Bring thread up where indicated on chart. Wrap floss once around needle, **Fig 4**, and reinsert needle close to where thread first came up. Hold wrapping thread tightly, close to surface of fabric. Pull needle through, letting thread go just as knot is formed. For a larger knot, use more strands of floss, but wrap only once.

Backstitch
Backstitches are worked after cross stitches have been completed. They may slope in any direction and are occasionally worked over more than one square of fabric. **Fig 5** shows the progression of several stitches; bring thread up at odd numbers and down at even numbers.

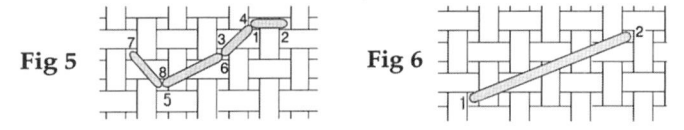

Straight Stitch
A straight stitch, **Fig 6**, is made like a long backstitch. Come up at one end of the stitch (1) and down at the other (2).

Couching
Couching is a technique where a straight stitch is held down at various points. The effect is a continuous line, but it is more secure than one long stitch. Follow chart for placement to make a straight stitch (1, 2). Then, at random intervals, bring needle up on one side of the stitch and down on the other side of the stitch in the same hole (A, B), **Fig. 7**. Repeat as needed. Intervals are not marked on the chart; make tacking stitches one inch (or less) apart.

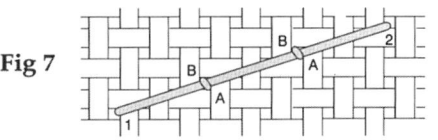

FINISHING
Wash stitched fabric in cool water with a gentle soap. Rinse well. Roll in a towel and squeeze out excess moisture. Place face down on a dry towel or padded surface and press carefully. Frame or finish as desired.

CHEETAH

Design size: 56 wide x 158 high
Cover model: stitched on a 13" x 20" piece of natural 14-count Aida cloth, shown matted in a 7-1/2" x 15" gold bamboo frame

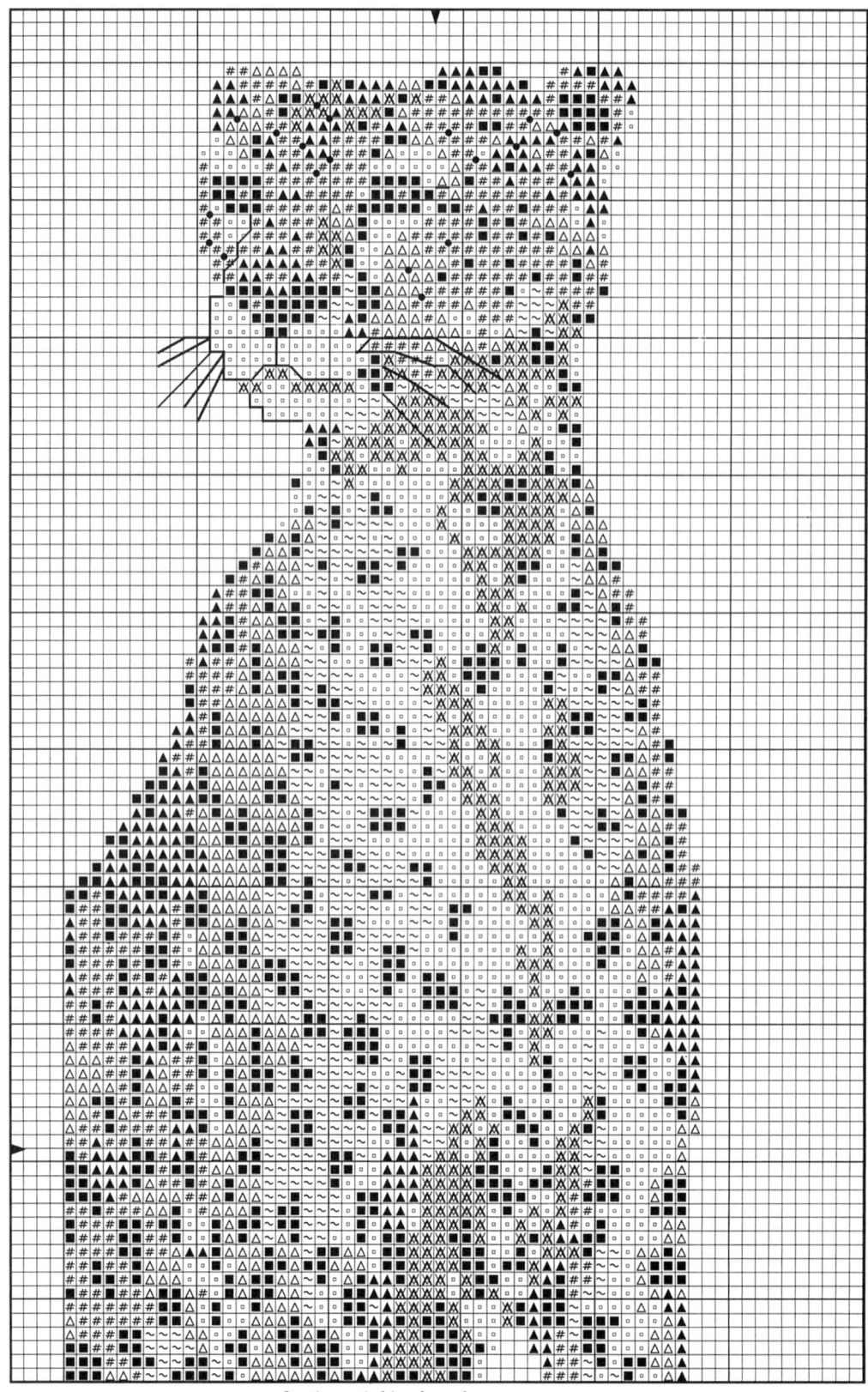

Continue stitching from chart on next page.

Shaded area shows last two rows in previous column.

	Anchor	Coats	DMC
▫ = white	2	1001	blanc
△ = lt gold	891	5363	676
# = med gold	901	2876	680
▲ = dk gold	365	5356	780
~ = tan	885	2386	739
★ = brown	889	5889	610
✕ = gray	831	5388	3782
■ = black	403	8403	310

• = French Knots: muzzle—black
\ = Straight Stitch: whiskers—gray
| = Backstitch:
   eye, nose, mouth—black

3

WILDLIFE ON PARADE

Design size: 350 wide x 95 high
Cover model: stitched on a 28" x 13" piece of ivory 16-count Aida cloth, shown in a 22" x 6-1/2" wood frame; if worked on 14-count fabric, the design will be larger

Note: The charts for this design are on pages 4, 5, 6, and 7.

Continue stitching from chart on page 5.

		Anchor	Coats	DMC			Anchor	Coats	DMC
▫	= white	1	1001	blanc	⟡	= dk tan	369	5347	435
♡	= med pink	27	3127	899	✕	= med rust	349	5309	3776
♥	= dk pink	42	3154	326	★	= dk rust	351	3340	400
✿	= orange	329	2327	3340	✎	= med brown	379	5379	840
∧	= yellow	306	2307	725	◆	= dk brown	360	5476	898
✘	= green	924	6845	730	△	= lt gray	899	5388	644
∪	= lt blue	976	7876	3752	#	= med gray	903	5393	640
✲	= dk blue	978	7978	312	▲	= dk gray	905	8500	3021
~	= lt tan	366	3335	951	■	= black	403	8403	310

• = French Knots:
  penguin, goose, elephant eyes—white
  remaining knots—black
\ = Straight Stitch: black (porcupine quills)
| = Backstitch:
  dk pink—flamingo body & legs, ostrich neck & legs

4

orange—bottoms of toucan and penguin beaks; beaks of flying birds, beak of bird on elephant
dk blue—1st flying bird wing feathers, ostrich body feathers, 2nd flying bird body (except wing feathers), body of bird on elephant
dk tan—top of zebra nose
med rust—ostrich beak, head of bird on elephant
dk rust—edge of pocket and between ears on kangaroo
med brown—camel, lower half of tiger, kangaroo, neck of 1st flying bird, monkey legs, giraffe, lion, upper body and legs of goose, deer (except face & inner leg)
dk gray—porcupine body, rhinoceros, 1st flying bird body & upper wings, goose breast, elephant
black—camel face, flamingo beak, upper half of tiger, toucan, penguin, top of penguin beak, kangaroo face, remainder of 1st flying bird, rhino nose, zebra, monkey, giraffe face, lion face & tip of tail, ostrich breast, remainder of 2nd flying bird, deer face outline & upper joint of foreleg, remainder of goose, remainder of bird on elephant, bear, turtle

	Anchor	Coats	DMC			Anchor	Coats	DMC
▫ = white	1	1001	blanc	✧ = dk tan		369	5347	435
♡ = med pink	27	3127	899	✕ = med rust		349	5309	3776
♥ = dk pink	42	3154	326	★ = dk rust		351	3340	400
✎ = orange	329	2327	3340	✐ = med brown		379	5379	840
∧ = yellow	306	2307	725	◆ = dk brown		360	5476	898
✖ = green	924	6845	730	△ = lt gray		899	5388	644
∽ = lt blue	976	7876	3752	# = med gray		903	5393	640
✱ = dk blue	978	7978	312	▲ = dk gray		905	8500	303
~ = lt tan	366	3335	951	■ = black		403	8403	310

• = French Knots:
  penguin, goose, elephant
  eyes—white
  remaining knots—black

\ = Straight Stitch: black
  (porcupine quills)

| = Backstitch:
  dk pink—flamingo body &
  legs, ostrich neck & legs

orange—bottoms of toucan and penguin beaks; beaks of flying birds, beak of bird on elephant
dk blue—1st flying bird wing feathers, ostrich body feathers, 2nd flying bird body (except wing feathers), body of bird on elephant
dk tan—top of zebra nose
med rust—ostrich beak, head of bird on elephant
dk rust—edge of pocket and between ears on kangaroo
med brown—camel, lower half of tiger, kangaroo, neck of 1st flying bird, monkey legs, giraffe, lion, upper body and legs of goose, deer (except face & inner leg)
dk gray—porcupine body, rhinoceros, 1st flying bird body & upper wings, goose breast, elephant
black—camel face, flamingo beak, upper half of tiger, toucan, penguin, top of penguin beak, kangaroo face, remainder of 1st flying bird, rhino nose, zebra, monkey, giraffe face, lion face & tip of tail, ostrich breast, remainder of 2nd flying bird, deer face outline & upper joint of foreleg, remainder of goose, remainder of bird on elephant, bear, turtle

PANTHER

Design size: 168 wide x 112 high
Cover model: stitched on a 21" x 17" piece of lt blue 14-count Aida cloth, shown matted in a 15" x 11" gold and black frame

Stitching notes: The combination of matte finish flower thread (using full cross stitches) and shiny 1/16" ribbon (using half cross stitches) creates the subtle play of light found on the coat of a stalking panther. If desired, other combinations of dull and shiny black threads can be used; full cross stitches will be required when substituting floss for 1/16" ribbon.

Unless otherwise directed, use two strands of floss or flower thread and one strand of 1/16" ribbon.

		Anchor	Coats	DMC
~	= lt purple	342	4303	211
◊	= med purple	109	4301	209
♦	= dk purple	110	4302	208
⊗	= blue-black	152	7160	939
+	= gold metallic			

Flower Thread
▫ = black   (3 skeins)

Balger 1/16" Ribbon
■ = blue-black half cross stitches   060
      (2 spools)

| = Backstitch:
   whiskers—blue-black floss (2 strands)
   back leg—black flower thread (3 strands)
   panther outline—1/16" ribbon (1 strand)

AFRICAN ZEBRA

Design size: 86 wide x 102 high
Cover model: stitched on a 16" x 16" piece of ivory 14-count Aida cloth, shown matted in a 10-1/2" x 10-1/2" patterned frame
Stitching note: You will need two skeins of black floss.

			Anchor	Coats	DMC
▫	=	white	1	1001	blanc
∧	=	tan	831	5388	3782
♡	=	lt brown	898	5898	370
♦	=	dk brown	906	5889	829
■	=	black	403	8403	310
|	=	Backstitch: black			

11

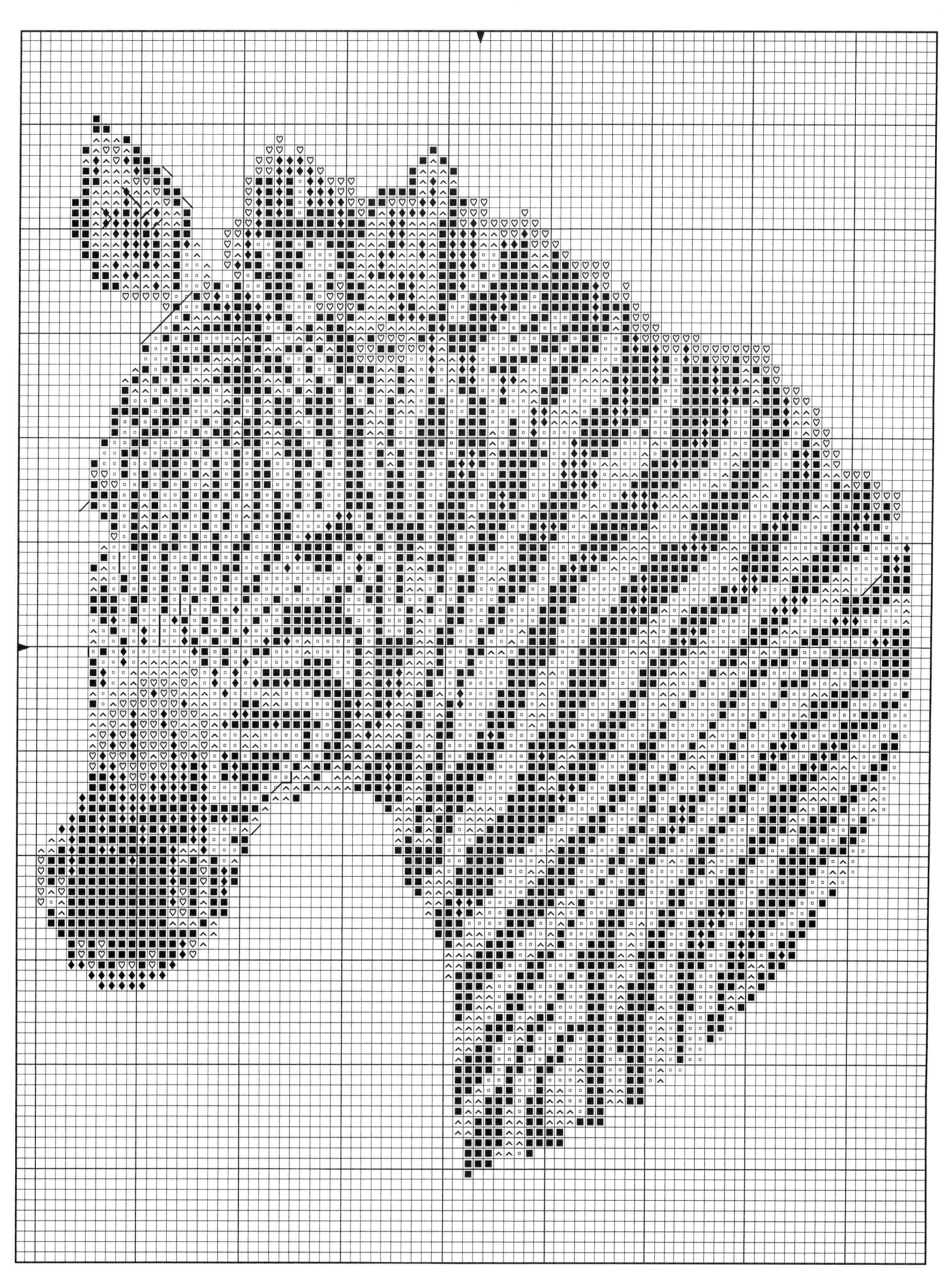

AMERICAN DEER

Design size: 85 wide x 105 high
Cover model: stitched on a 16" x 16" piece of ivory 14-count Aida cloth, shown matted in an 11" x 11" wood frame

		Anchor	Coats	DMC
▫ =	white	1	1001	blanc
× =	gold	374	5374	420
✎ =	rust	347	5347	402
△ =	lt brown	367	5375	945
# =	med brown	936	5936	632
▲ =	dk brown	380	5477	938
■ =	black	403	8403	310
| =	Backstitch: black			

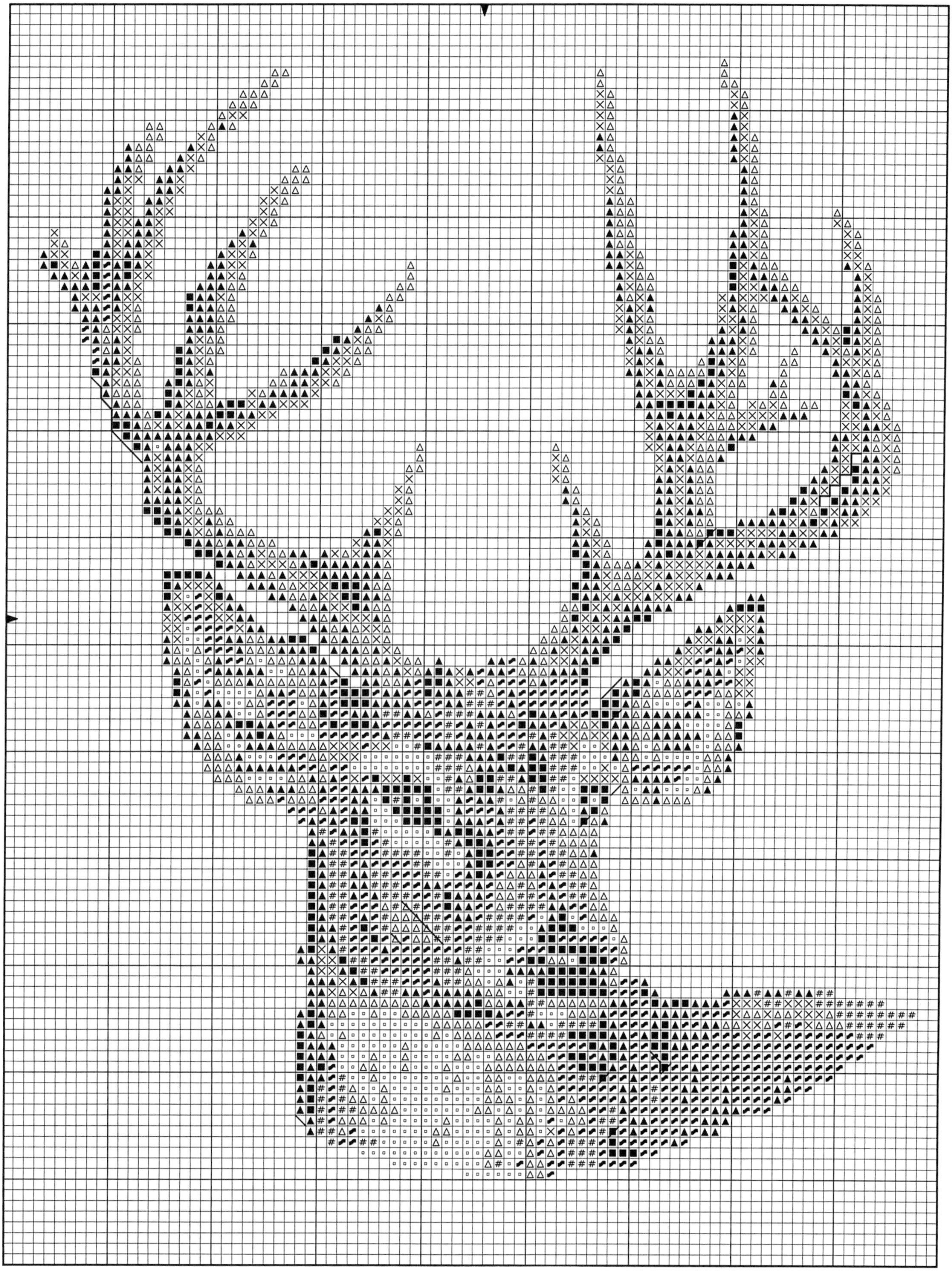

MARGAY

Design size: 101 wide x 92 high
Cover model: stitched on a 16" x 16" piece of ivory 14-count Aida cloth, shown matted in a 10" x 10" black frame

14

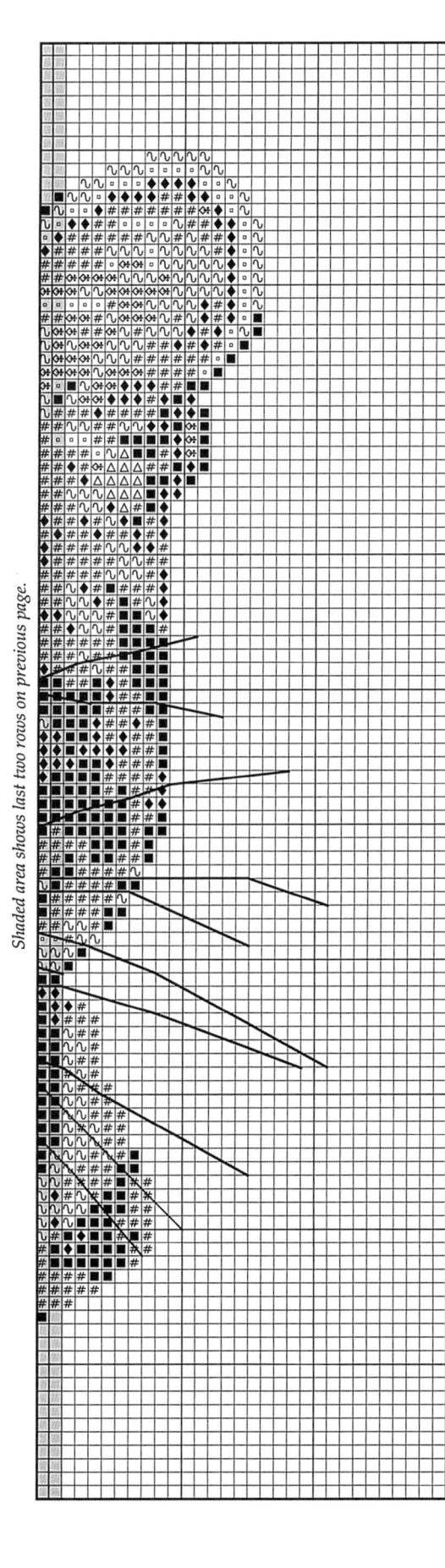

Shaded area shows last two rows on previous page.

	Anchor	Coats	DMC
▫ = white	1	1001	blanc
✸ = pink	9575	3868	3341
∩ = peach	373	5350	422
△ = rust	370	5356	434
# = med brown	889	5889	610
♦ = dk brown	905	8500	303
■ = black	403	8403	310

- • = French Knots:
  nose—white
  muzzle—black
- ⊸ = Couching:
  whiskers—white
- \ = Straight Stitch:
  eye—white
- | = Backstitch:
  pupils—dk brown
  iris, nose, mouth—black

15

PANDA

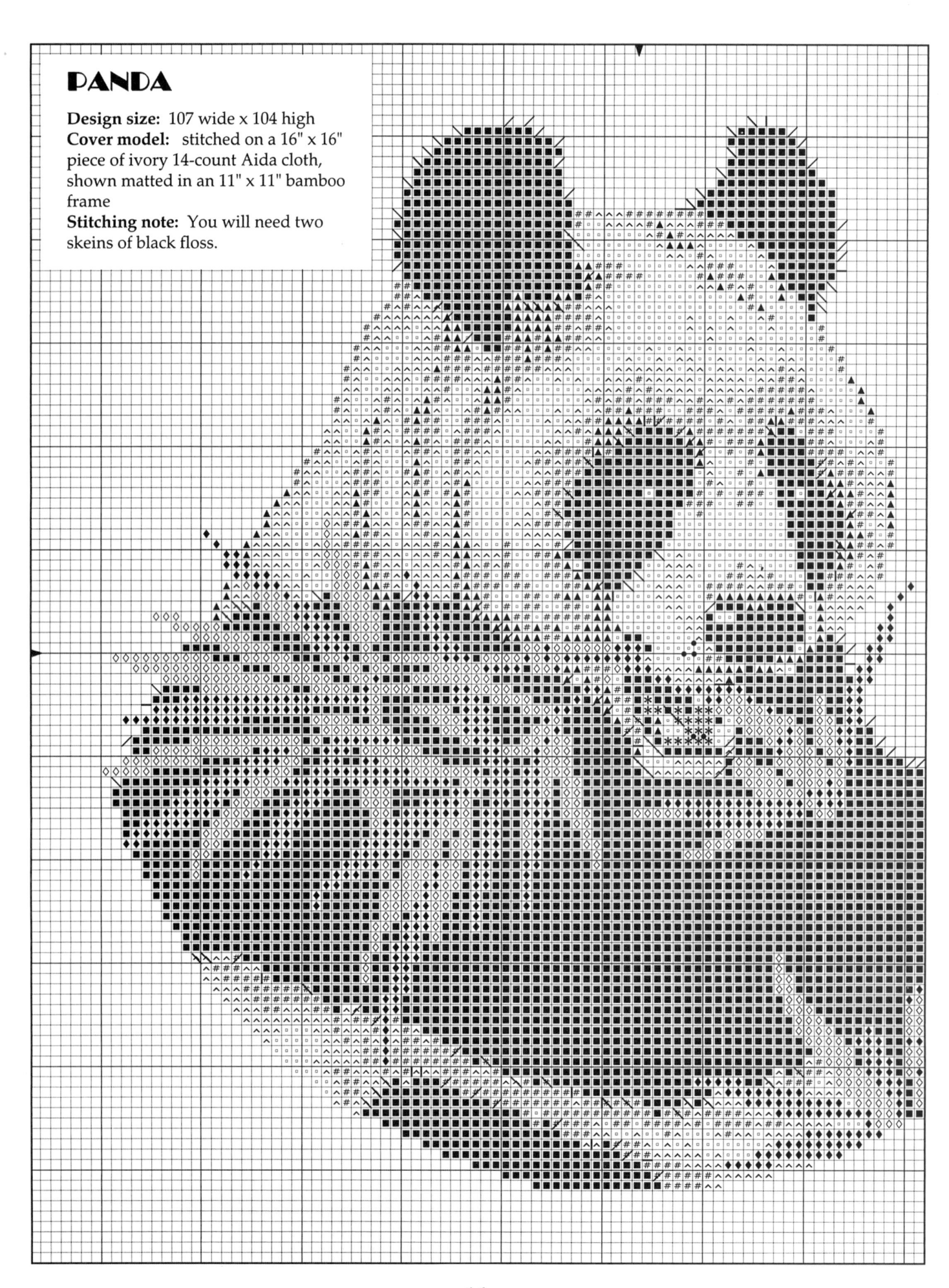

Design size: 107 wide x 104 high
Cover model: stitched on a 16" x 16" piece of ivory 14-count Aida cloth, shown matted in an 11" x 11" bamboo frame
Stitching note: You will need two skeins of black floss.